A flower surrounded by concrete can still flourish, it can still bloom no matter its surroundings

it takes what it needs to survive

Mother nature will always prevail

As I sat there I thought I needed to capture this to prove no matter what you're going through in life, be a flower and stand out even if you're surrounded by stuff that tries to keep you down and stuck. Your surroundings are just surroundings flourish, grow and be the best possible version of yourself you can.

I LOOK FOR CROWS AND MOTHS INSTEAD OF RAINBOWS AND FEATHERS

WITHOUT THE DARK WE DON'T KNOW THE LIGHT AND WITHOUT THE LIGHT WE WOULDNT KNOW THE DARK BALANCE IN LIFE IS KEY

She whispers secrets to the wind and hangs onto the lullabies of the trees
Her hands are numb as she realizes everything she desires is in reach

Tranquility a place that's bliss
The waves crashing the bitter sea air against my face
The powerful element of water shaping the rocks it's so peaceful
i don't even want to write just bask in the peaking sun
Enjoy the silence enjoy the moment be mindful the clouds look so
surreal like a painted picture perfectly created in the sky i wonder
what creatures lurk in the salty waters beyond the depths of a no
mans land deep breaths in and out its like purification entering
my lungs i smile and feel content my bodys recharged

I GOT GIVEN A FLOWER THIS ISN'T JUST ANY FLOWER THIS IS A GIFT OFF MY
CHILD THIS IS MORE THAN A FLOWER THIS IS MUMMY/DADDY THIS IS SO
PRETTY AND I'M GIVING IT TO YOU MUMMY/DADDY I LOVE YOU
A CHILD SEES BEAUTY WHICH WE ONCE SAW THEY SEE NO WRONG IN THE
WORLD AT SUCH A YOUNG AGE THEY SEE A WORLD FULL OF EXPLORATION A
THIRST TO KNOW AND TO ENGAGE A FLOWER IS NOT JUST A FLOWER ACCEPT
THIS GIFT AND WATCH THEM GROW GET DOWN IN THE MUD AND LOOK FOR
BUGS SHHH BE CAREFUL NOT TO WAKE THE FAIRIES FOR THEY TAKE CARE OF THE
GREEN GRASS AND THE FLOWERS THAT GROW ENJOY MAKING POTIONS AND
CONCOCTIONS REMEMBER WHAT IT'S LIKE DIG INTO THE REALM OF YOUR
IMAGINATION

As I lay down wings cover me with a warm embrace its safe here I tell myself her soft touch against my face and the silk against my legs a pink shimmer covers me like I'm sat in a bubble but I can't move else it will pop so I lay silently and stare blankly at the wall then I look down and see her wings have the same colour and pattern as my duvet her white soft silky gown is my bed sheet and her body is the base of my bed the bubble pops can I please just call it my angel after all it feels like heaven my wings my savior my bed

I FALL DOWN BUT I ALSO COME BACK AND FLY HIGHER THAN BEFORE IF I HAVE TO START OVER AGAIN I WILL DO WITH MORE WISDOM MORE STRENGTH AND WITH MY DIGNITY INTACT NEVER UNDERESTIMATE THE STRENGTH OF SOMEONE WITH A MENTAL ILLNESS WE ARE NOT HOW SOCIETY DEFINES US AND HERE I AM STRIVING USING TRAUMATIC EXPERIENCES THE PAIN AS FUEL TO STAND UP AND SHOUT I GOT THIS

POSITIVITY IS EASY WHEN YOU KNOW HOW TO DISTANCE YOURSELF FROM THE NEGATIVITY,BE KIND, HELP PEOPLE AND EVEN IF YOU DON'T RECEIVE IT BACK YOU ARE KIND YOU ARE A NICE PERSON THEY CAN CUSS YOU AND TRY AND DRAG YOU DOWN, THAT'S THEIR PROBLEM NOT URES STAY KIND HELP PEOPLE!! STAY TRUE TO YOU!! MAKE PEOPLE LAUGH,STAY STRONG AND CARRY ON

No furry baby sleeping next to my shoulder
Water bowl still full and tapped turnt off
No scratching at night in the litter box
I used to say he was digging for China because of the noise and how
much he scratched so much
No more morning meows
No more nuzzling my face
Sat patiently waiting looking at me for a tap on my lap to say
"come on"
No more sneaking Under the dinner table waiting for some
chicken to be chucked
No more fur balls
These are things I miss so much
No more chasing the tape measure
No more meowing at the bathroom door
No more headbutts to say I love you
No more diary who always listened who do I hug now when life
feels like a mission
You've seen me happy you've seen me hurt you've soaked in my
tears and given me laughter you showed me love so pure you've
seen me break and get back up again you've been my comfort when
my heart was broken my ickle secret diary my first baby my fur baby

What is freedom what is peace of mind,
Is it ones state of thoughts or manifested self help cure that you
have to find,
Is it a walk in nature or a seat by the sea
is it the feeling of euphoria and serenity
do you have to see it or can you just believe
Can you think outside with no box required and be in harmony
Is it art drawing or writing expressing that individual creativity
Is it passion that no one else can feel
Is it your family and friend's hugs that fills you with compassion
that eases the chaos in your loud mind
Is it your children that bring so much joy into your life
Is it meeting a stranger giving them all your trust
Is it avoiding strife and being kind
understanding the sorrow in their eyes
Is Supercalifragilisticexpialidocious Mary Poppins right?
What is freedom what is peace of mind

Relationships are like flowers if you love flowers why pick it from the ground you know it will die but you go home and try nurture it and put it in a vase hoping it will still be alive 2 mora when you wake but there's still a gut feeling i've picked it no matter what you try to do to keep it alive you taking it away from its natural habitat i've tried making it grow whilst taking all the good away from it and no matter how much food or water u give it its withering away as each day goes on its strength weakens it falls down each day so moral of the story is if you love something leave it be trying to change their habitat and what there used to will only end up in negativity if you leave it alone you will you can still see it everyday and watch it bloom and that will make you more happier than watching it die a little everyday

She loved how she loved
Her mind,body,and soul
Ow how she loved you should know
A Queen with her perfect grown
She built you up as you tear her down
A joker amongst the pack
Never really knew love it was just a laugh
He stole her heart and buried it with the ace of spades
He never drew a Queen before she wasn't afraid
Ow how she loved with all her heart
Asking her to wait whilst u re shuffle and play the game!!
She treated you like a king and loved your flaws and all
Ow how she loved and he never loved at all it's a shame
Now the Queen has a hand in play
Whilst she threw down what used to be a king to the rest of a pile she
smiled as Magic appeared within the deck when she threw down the
King she thought hung on a sec! For the King to turn into a joker
no longer did she have to suffer for she is no longer going to wait
tired of the hand in play she places the cards down and says I fold
cause even if she did win this shits to old!

It's all about fast cars and big houses and who's got the latest gifts and gadgets. all about technology and the future of a well paid job but if this didn't exist what Would we be doing What would be fun, what would we be creating? Not something we are gonna ruin would we create a happy stable place for our children or would we spending more time outside and not moaning would we be able to think for ourselves would we have a new world order if we took internet out the equation are we getting brainwashed to think were becoming more smart cause the technology has been upgraded how many of you have sat down and wrote a letter and not been able to spell because you're so used to having predictive text how many of you have lost your phone and got angry because you feel like you lost something important when really what's important is your family friends and your children

HOW MANY OF YOU HAVE SAT THERE WHILST YOUR KIDS ARE TALKING AND YOU'RE SAT THERE WITH YOUR PHONE IN YA HAND AND YOU SAY YES TO WHATEVER THERE ASKING BECAUSE YOURE TO WRAPPED UP IN A CONVERSATION THAT PROBABLY IS ABOUT TALKING ABOUT OTHERS WHEN A CHILD IS SAT THERE LEARNING FROM EXAMPLES AND WHEN YOU TELL THEM THEY CAN'T PLAY ON THERE CONSOLE CAUSE YOU SAID SO BUT SIT THERE STILL WITH YOUR PHONE IN YOUR HAND LEADING BY EXAMPLE!! HAVE YOU TAKEN A WALK THIS WEEK AND TALKED TO YOUR CHILD ABOUT NATURE CAUSE MAYBE ONE DAY THAT IS ALL THAT'S GONNA BE LEFT BECAUSE THERE WILL ALWAYS BE ANIMALS AND PLANTS AND THE OUTDOORS BUT TECHNOLOGY MIGHT NOT ALWAYS BE THERE!! JUST A REMINDER

What a beautiful day the sun is shining
is it really such a beautiful day when you have a black cloud that
hovers above your head soaking up every bit of negativity that
surrounds you but then it gets to heavy and then cracks appear the
demons then slowly creep out but only you can hear
they darken your day whilst you're awake your very own
nightmare that you can't escape
but you still look up at the sky and say "what a beautiful day" you
smile and wave at people and say you have a good day too yeah mate
I'm all good yeah everything's fine! you get home your safety place
you search the house for a release and escape a taste!!
You sit there grasping on to a glass of water and all The medicine
you can find you sit there staring at the one solution to all your
problems all you can hear IT'S THE ONLY WAY the demons are getting
louder and starting to speak you grip your hair and you scream
cause your battling between dark and light then your phone lights
up and you see a txt then you see your children's smiles on your
screen cover!! Then a lightbulb appears and a voice SAYS DON'T YOU
DARE FUCKING GIVE UP!!!

Sometimes you have to write your own ending!!! It's a book that you thought you could read till the end but the truth is you're stuck on same chapter same sentences trying to understand trying to visualise it trying to reach the end your fingertips are wearing out the ink on the pages because your holding onto that one chapter when your just going to be stuck going around in circles same chapter different day

Even the positive people get stuck in a negative rut now and then but that's okay because as long as you acknowledge it and know where the negativity is coming from and address it that in itself is a strength

Never let anyone bring you down stand up tall stand your ground be your self be real you have your own identity live life with music in your heart
If your not happy then that's the place to start this is a poem not me tryin to mc p.s my freind never let anyone mess you up mentally
This is what anxiety looks like I look happy and cosy I look comfortable but in my head there's a demon who's trying to knock on the door shall I open it shall I let him in shall I slam that door on his face shall I find my happy place
which is my Cosy look!!

She's resting bitch faceShe's horrible and doesn't want you to leave your house. She wants you all to herself!!
She hates you having other friends
She makes you feel worthless and ugly
She makes you stay drained and down
She calls you every name under the sun
But you forgive her because she's always there for you
She makes you walk the long way around to the shop so u don't speak to anyone She controls you "SHE" ———IS ANXIETY ——It's a controlling relationship right??
A relationship that's more toxic than a Normal relationship but she won't let you have a relationship because "SHE IS THE ONLY ONE WHO UNDERSTANDS"
She won't let you walk away because even though she's toxic she's always there! A TOXIC RELATIONSHIP YOU HAVE TO END!! Hats off to anyone who suffers with this " BITCH" because it's a hard one to let go of

My beauty comes from owning my own style!! I am perfect in my
own imperfections
I'm unique that's what makes my soul shine bright
My unique alternative different ways will never go out of taste
because everything I like will never go out of my style
I know who I am inside and out I'm art I wear my story on my
skin you won't understand it but it doesn't matter because I do
and it's meaningful to me
I don't pretend to be something I ain't I wear my "weird"
"funny" "beautiful " "alternative" "kindness" "crazy ass" "no
filtered mouth"
Crown with pride! I am MissQueenNt

WORD'S WE CLING ONTO WORDS IF I'VE LEARNT ANYTHING IN THE LAST COUPLE OF MONTHS IT'S WORDS MEAN NOTHING I COULD GO UP TO A STRANGER ON THE STREET AND SAY I LOVE YOU IT WOULDN'T MEAN FUCK ALL I DON'T LOVE THEM, BUT I CAN EASILY SAY IT!! SOMEONE CAN TELL YOU ALL THE RIGHT THINGS ALL THE I'M SORRY,I LOVE YOU,ALL THE SWEET NOTHINGS YOU WANT TO HEAR BUT DOESN'T MEAN IT'S THE TRUTH, YOU GET TOLD BY THE DOCKS YOU'RE ILL AND YOU BELIEVE THEM RIGHT BECAUSE OF THEIR PROFESSION YOU GET TOLD ABOUT ALL THIS BAD NEWS ON THE TV AND YOU BELIEVE IT HIS IS HOW POWERFUL SOME WORDS CAN BE ANYONE CAN TELL YOU ANYTHING IT'S THERE ACTIONS THAT'S SPEAKS NOT THERE WORDS IF SOMEONE'S IS SORRY THEY WOULDN'T CONTINUALLY KEEP DOING IT IF SOMEONE TRULY LOVES YOU THEY WOULD RESPECT YOU NEVER BE SORRY FOR TELLING SOMEONE HOW YOU FEEL THEY HAVE NO RIGHT TO TELL YOU IT'S NOT TRUE BECAUSE IT'S YOU'RE FEELINGS THEY CAN'T ARGUE WITH THAT!! ACTIONS SHOW LOVE ACTIONS SHOW THE I'M SORRY PROMISES ARE MADE TO BE KEPT NOT BROKEN IF YOU CAN'T KEEP A PROMISE THEN DON'T SAY IT NOT EVERYONE WILL SHOW YOU THEY ACTUALLY GIVE A FUCK BUT CAN SAY IT TILL THERE BLUE IN THE FACE TRUST ACTIONS TRUST YOU'RE OWN INSTINCTS!! IT'S NOT YOUR JOB TO MAKE SOMEONE ELSE HAPPY, IT'S YOUR JOB TO MAKE YOURSELF HAPPY. ALWAYS WATCH SOMEONE'S ACTIONS THAT'S THE KEY!

You can give someone a rope and they might take an inch they might blind you they might use it to lean upon like the ropes around the ring but if you give them some thread you can tell them to sew their own fucking rope and get a grip!

I have a hole in my heart that is not visible to see can't see it with your eyes but it feels visible to me When your feet are heavy and your shoulders wear you down, when you miss them and all you feel is pain walking with a frown

When the world feels different and it's never going to be the the same, try and hold onto the hope and the light try to remember how to fight

Go for a walk or scream and cry do what makes you feel better, but remember to shine, though you may never feel like the pain will go away and everything is hard

Cherish the memories that live inside you don't throw your cards even though the seasons will come and go

Your memory will live on never fade it will show I am your daughter and you my father I love and miss you so much wish you could of stayed

Life is giving me reasons to crumble struggling through lockdown, trying to stay afloat trying to stay positive and wear my crown, 2020 has taken my freedom and rights it's taken my father and it's taken my animal soulmate but I will stand up and fight, fight through the sorrow and pain fight through the sadness of today

A world where everyone's feeling not as ease I get up every morning and that's a start for me

Depression wants me to stay in bed my mentality the mess in my head but I'm a born survivor a prem baby from day one

I'm raising a queen and king no folding for me, I will keep climbing through this quicksand trying to get me to sink me the bottom trying to suffocate me with every day obstacles

Hear me roar I'm a mother and I'm made of material thats hardcore

I will dig deep and find the strength to carry on day by day one foot in front of the other

I will prevail in a world that wants me to fail.

Sometimes you wake and thoughts fill your head
It's frustrating trying to explain my thoughts haven't got a diary
they just slot themselves in
Darkness creeps in!! Tip toeing at my door but I won't let that
mother fucker in anymore
I've slammed that door on his face
So if I'm quite do not take offence
Silence is something I'm not familiar with
I'm trying to control the loudness in my head I'm trying to battle
I look content but I'm battling a fight you wouldn't ever
understand
Just leave me to be silent leave me be if you can

Caged in my thoughts consumed Reality or a dimension to dive in
Rushing around like a bee trapped in a glass
The noise is to loud I will just laugh
Don't recognise the person in the mirror I guess I should clean it
for it to be more clearer Mascara stained eyes and foundation
streaked mark's Time goes to fast when you're wondering what to
do My mind doesn't stay quiet but I'm quite to you
Hearts racing like the grand national sound
It's all I can feel as I lay my hand on chest as it pounds
An intruder has broken in today. It's raining so I don't have to
go out so I'm okay! Are u okay the question I really never ask
I'm to busy with life and making my kids happy and laugh
My hands are dry from all the cleaning that has to be done
Mummy take a break let's have some fun But escaping these
programmed wires that are electronically running threw my brain
I think I need a sleep but that's selfish to say Doing everything on
my own is taking a toll But I'm a happy healer an empath so it
won't show I will make you laugh and build you up
I will try my best to not tell you what's up
I've wiped the mirror but I still can't see I just wanna recognise
the person standing in front of me

People can change with the pain they feel
Hurt makes me people look within themselves and it won't heal
When you lose control of your emotions and your heart it makes
you realise what's important not games and tit for tat it also
makes you stronger inside when you step back and analyse the
situation without the fear without feeling you've lost control you
bring to the surface the truth your own faults you're own ways you
need to change and that's how pain plays a bit part in change! Cause
you'll do anything in your Power once you've felt that pain to
never feel that pain again there for nothing but growth and
strength can come from it!! Pain is also a positive it just depends
on how as you as a person looks at it

I was late I don't mean I missed the time and place I was meant to be at, but I was late,late waking up late on my morning routine, bound by the man made machine that ticks so loud in my head and screams YOU ARE LATE!! Then approaches panic I was behind schedule, here it comes the all mighty and all powerful mind fuck of all ANXIETY!! Running around my body doing what it seems Lap's and lap's my head my skin my heart my chest and finally my lungs, I was late I was behind schedule, panic and anxiety are best friends they work so well together moulded and entwined like water filling a cup,taking any shape or form! I was late I was behind schedule, after tackling what seems to be a t-rex shaped like form of a toddler I walked out the door on time, I was at the school gates on time, I told panic and anxiety goodbye have a nice day because I got there now panic and anxiety were still there but so was logic and understanding, and thank god so was my higher consciousness, Flew in like superman puffed out there chest and said " WE ARE HERE AND WE ARE POWERFUL" I jumped in my car and my higher power took me I chilled I relaxed I let them take over and I breathed I smiled I wasn't late,, my mind told me I was the man made machine that grabs everyone and sucks them in, the ticking was quite the screams went away and I set myself up for a positive day

I'VE GOT MY BEAUTY I'VE GOT GRACE I'VE GOT MY DAUGHTER TO PUT A SMILE ON MY FACE I'VE GOT MY SON WHO ALWAYS MAKES ME LAUGH I'VE GOT FAMILY AND FRIENDS AND WHATS LAST IS I STILL GOT MY HEART TO BARE EVEN WHEN THE WORLD WANTS TO BRING YOU DOWN LOOK UP AT THE SKY RAIN OR SHINE SAY THANKYOU TO THE UNIVERSE FOR MAKING ME REALISE I CAN BE ME ALTERNATIVE CRAZY BAT OF SHIT AND THANK YOU FOR BLESSING ME WITH SOMEONE WHO GAVE ME A BEAUTIFUL GIFT BECAUSE EVEN THOUGH THE LOVE HAS GONE I WILL ALWAYS HAVE THIS LITTLE LADY AND MY SON WHO LOOKS UP TO ME AND DEPENDS ON ME

WHO MADE UP THE WORD "HAPPINESS" IN THE VIKINGS TIMES WAS CALLED "FORTUNATE" A HOMELESS MAN'S PERSPECTIVE ON HAPPINESS IS A HOME, A BED, FOOD AND A ROOF OVER HIS HEAD!! A RICH MAN'S PERSPECTIVE ON HAPPINESS IS POWER AND MONEY THEREFORE NEITHER OF THEM WILL REALLY UNDERSTAND HAPPINESS IT'S A "STATE OF MIND" THE WORD HAPPINESS WAS MAN MADE FOR THE EMOTIONS THAT WE ARE FEELING YOU SMILE YOU'RE HAPPY BUT HAPPINESS IS A PEACEFUL STATE OF MIND YOU CAN PEACEFUL AND NOT SMILE OR LAUGH, YOU CAN BE FORTUNATE BUT NOT BE HAPPY HAPPINESS HAS A LOT TO ANSWER FOR!!! WE ALL LOOK FOR HAPPINESS IN MATERIALISTIC THINGS WE BUY BECAUSE THAT GIVES A "JOY" FEELING IT MAKES US SMILE BUT IT'S NOT TRUE HAPPINESS, WE ARE ALL LOOKING TO BE HAPPY BUT IF YOUR CONTENT AND AT PEACE WITH YOURSELF THAT IS YOUR OWN HAPPINESS YOU CAN BE SAD AND PEACEFUL SO THEREFORE SURELY YOU'RE HAPPY WHEN YOU'RE ALSO SAD BECAUSE YOUR PEACEFUL!!! SO IT DOESN'T MATTER WHAT EMOTION YOU'RE FEELING, IF YOU'RE SEARCHING FOR HAPPINESS, BEING AT PEACE WITHIN YOURSELF, HAPPINESS IS NOT SOMETHING YOU FIND, IT'S A STATE OF MIND!!

Do I regret giving people chance after chance NO I'm the one with a good heart enough to see the good in everyone that's a gift not a curse Now what I need to learn is to protect myself know that I don't have to let them in Would I change the heartache and the pain of not feeling like am enough NO Because I've been giving a beautiful gift from the universe and her name is Luna

Moon princess needs me loves me unconditionally she can't live without me Do I regret building someone up and then they vanish NO because at that moment in time I also needed help and this was meant to happen I'm a helper and a healer I will always help people see their true potential I just have to learn how to not let them drain my energy and not give them all of me Do I regret this pain NO it makes me realise I am not a cold hearted bitch I am someone who feels and I will not stay quiet when I have a voice Do I feel like a mug NO what's the point there problems is not my problems there mind I can not fix

I won't settle for less, Im building strong grounds for my prince and princess so they grow up knowing their worth to, haven't got no time for half hearted love and agendas I'm a empress I know what I deserve

Craving it just your touch just your presence,need your love I need to hear your voice I'm all alone and I feel like I can't breathe you're letting me break your letting me fall!
You need your space I need it all
I wanna be by your side when your weak I wanna be the one u turn to when u feel like u can't see
I will guide you I will lead u be free but if I'm not getting it back we just cannot be

FULL OF LIFE HER EYES SAW DIFFERENTLY SHE DIDN'T SEE THE TOYS OR THE
DOLLS ON THE FLOOR
SHE SAW THE SUN'S RAYS SHINING ON THE WALL
SHE CAN SEE ENERGY AND FEELS SO MUCH LOVE
SHE WANTS TO KNOW EVERYTHING

HE INTRIGUES ME,
I WONDER WHAT HIS EYES HAVE SEEN,
BUT YET HE LOOKS AT ME WITH A GENTLE STARE
HE HOLDS ME WITH LOVE HIS ARMS ARE LIKE SHACKLES OF LIGHT, GUARDING
MY SOUL EVEN THOUGH HIS HANDS CARRY HEAVY BURDENS OF THE PAST,
HIS WORDS SO CALMING AND MAKE ME FEEL AT EASE HIS GENTLE TONGUE
THAT SOOTHES MY VOICE
HIS KISS HIS GENTLE LIPS WHEN THEY TOUCH MINE FEELS LIKE OUR SOULS
INTWINE ARE FUCKING EACH OTHER'S SOULS!! HIS ENERGY FLOWS SO POSITIVE
AND FREE HE JUST DOESN'T SEE ME HE TRULY SEES ME

LOVE IS A POWERFUL THING IN THE WRONG HANDS IN CAN LEAD TO HATE

If you channel Love properly and allow it to flow it can be greatness It changes you this thing called love Some people try changing the person they "fell in love with" the person who they once adored and their flaws The thing that made them love that person But also people change when there "in love" once you get this thing called love it can be cruel you can love unconditionally even the bad bits One thing I've learnt about love is it can fuck you up worse then any drug known to man Because when your in love you have no control your heart just won't let them go That's you're addiction fills your veins and once it's intoxicating you you want more you're scared of it leaving you or hurting you cause the worse pain is recovery allowing it to go allowing it to leave your veins when it's been in your stream for years You feel it physically break your heart and soul you let out the tearsn but only you know the story that life has dealt you No one really knows how u feel cause each love is different on a different scale like mentally it gets a hold of your soul it can make you or break you only you can decide how you want to treat love! Once you've let it turn into hate you're just projecting hate So the best thing to do is even if breaks give you love and more love cause at least you can say you projected love and you have lots of love to give!

Favourite day of the week is Tuesdays home cooked food flat always smells lovely it smells like home a listen ear and support she has no clue how much she means to me I might have lost who I thought was the love of my life but I gained love the love that comes from a nan can never be replaced you can see how much wisdom she holds inside always love listening to her stories of what life was like back when she was little her hugs comfort me she may be stuck in her ways but I love her and wouldn't have it another way

She never judges me no matter what I say even the hardest things i never want to say but i feel comfortable and i know i can tell her anything she guides me through the darkest days always there to listen and to help always make sure our bellies are full and we have clothes on our backs she loves us unconditionally and we lover loads

This feeling rushing through me
Can't explain what it is Trying to hide my heart but I can't resist
Ure kind and a good soul ure heart is made up of pure gold
But deep down I get a bad feeling,a feeling that u also know, Scared
and afraid to open up, Scared of commitment people say I love u to
much, Not many really know the truth,the true meaning of saying
I love you What if u hurt me what if I'm not enough,what if u go
behind my back cause u say u always fuck things up,
What if I can't keep u grounded and strong,
What if we're mentally gonna fuck each other cause that's all I've
known I love the feeling wen ure around But I also hate feeling of
a broken heart that I can't stand, I'm done with crying and
letting people break me Fed up of failing relationships and not
being able to call someone my soul mate my baby I want it to be
right and dont wanna rush I wanna make sure ure committed like
me Just as much Love isn't about words and physical stuff It's about
energy and connection and jealousy and anger and lust it's
greed. And it's envy. It is the seven deadly sins I don't want the
negatives only the positive I wanna connect with you on a whole
new level Wanna feel your spiritual vibes wanna see into your soul
wanna build a strong foundation that only we will know!!

Your mind is the most precious thing you can own a powerful tool on its own,if in the wrong state it can manipulate,but it can teach calmness and to be at peace,and be great,in a world full of bad vibes it can be used to capture memories and good times,control your mind so it doesn't do u wrong,it isn't other people who hurt u and do u wrong it's your own mind that makes u think that's what u deserve so u attract it and u end up getting hurt, don't be ashamed to walk away from the negativity if it's making u think so wrongly,who cares what other people think,u need to do stuff for yourself for your mentality,and your kids if you have them,don't get caught up in a world full of a negative cycle,be you be free be unstoppable,watch the positivity flow thru your veins and watch the haters hate

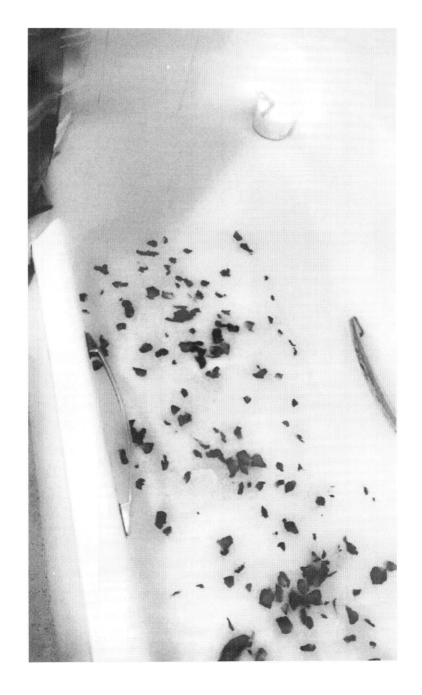

No filter!! Why do we feel ugly without a filter? Why do we feel the need to mask our blemishes?,our beautiful own perfect imperfections, why do we feel insecure? Why do we let media make us feel ugly? for not having perfect skin a perfect shaped face and perfect teeth the perfect smile, we all have our own insecurities about ourselves that's called being human

Beauty is not defined by our looks, it's defined by our souls and heart. A filter might be able to cover up our blemishes but we can't filter our souls fall in love with someone's soul the deed's they do! as the saying goes beauty fades but our soul never grows old

I'm becoming to love and understand why I'm different,why I attract people Into my life that need guidance,I understand I have a gift,I have a purpose,I'm not a perfect woman who's been photoshopped!!,I don't have perfect hair,teeth or a perfect body I'm not a saint, but I know I have a heart and soul, I'm a healer but I'm not taking anymore patients I have two close friends and a family that love me and most of all I have two incredible children to raise I have unconditional love

I feel the cold air upon my skin
It makes me shiver
for once I was numb
And negativity tried to enter
I feel my aching body
I feel the deep breaths as I yawn
I feel tired but not no more torn
I feel lighter I felt called
The sun warms me up
And the sea calms me down
The waves it's Like there communicating in there own special way
sea air cleanses my mind and soul
Just the beauty and the Tranquility of it all
I sit and I embrace the energy all around
I remember that I have this crown

Chains broken, sword has been pulled, powers returned to which it once was cold, reborn with clear new vision, asleep for so long but now my potential has risen, This goddess witch no longer in slumber, arise warrior and take your position , A free spirit who can't be Tamed a dragons heart she holds with no name , fierce and fiery with a soft heart who is bold, braver than any heart she imprints on braver than anyone you know.

Im a single mother and the days are full of stress i don't get a break or a bubble bath and have a break, feel like i'm on call 24/7 hours a day some days i have to force myself up out of bed just to start the day i love them both more than anyone knows but still why do i feel guilty for wanting some time alone why do i just want to chill and do nothing at home always busy and never a rest there both so special but some days it is tough

A tear ran down my cheek I couldn't stop it just let it flow naturally but then came the uncontrollable crying I've lost two important connections in my life and I'm trying boy am I trying, trying to fight everyday obstacles whilst grieving feels impossible I feel like a failure I feel like a fraud but I'm still breathing so much pain consumes me but I still laugh and smile some days are good and some days I want to give up but I'm battling on through this life of tough love see when your strong you feel guilty for being weak you've got to get up everyday and pretend your okay and stand tall on those two feet when in actual fact you feel like you can't go on and people tell you to see the positivity but how can you when grieving it's not easy what's positive about losing a father and your family cat how can I overcome this how do I get back back my whole mind frame it all has changed the whole concept of reality and every day life has been lifted and I see in new ways the worlds darker and colder every single day I don't like this process of emotions that's took hold I'm angry at the person leaving because I loved them so much more then they will know and now I will never hear there voice or feel there touch there hugs there wisdom that gave me strength every day I will wipe away my tears and pretend I'm okay.

There laughs brighten up my day even if i don't want to smile children they have a way a way to make you feel love even when lifes tough they give you a smile or a hug and its pure love being a parent isn't always easy especially when you feeling like you've got no energy it's easy to fall into this negative rut and always moan and stress but it won't solve anything just take five minutes and rest and try and reprogramme your mind is it worth it is stressing over the smallest of things worth the energy instead of losing your mind try and think differently if the children are loud at least there happy if they spill something on the floor don't moan just clean it up with a smile on your face see the thing we forget is how it made us feel when our parents got upset when we were young accidents happen and words we can't take back be a child forget the stress and have a laugh

Bags in his hands with no explanation the door slams and his footsteps echoed around the concrete hallway her hands full of tears she promised herself she wouldn't cry anymore the amount of tears she's shed for him could fill an ocean

It's easy to let someone walk all over you especially when you see the good in them you're always telling yourself they can change because deep down inside you can see the caring side but that's not enough someone will not change unless they want to no matter what you do, its themselves that have to see the light stuck in there cycle until the lightbulb goes bright some people like to be negative and moan all the time because for them it's how they get attention they cling onto the sorrow and pain and let it consume them and they live like that from day to day there happy and let it run through there veins clucking for there next fix or they constantly bring up the pass and cant move on and let it go I feel sorrow for them I really do

They are not the same anymore an evil
Disease has taken over there soul they have no empathy for anyone
they've lost the spark that once ignited the flame sold their soul
for a bag of brown or white all their thoughts are stuck on their
next fix discouraging family members loved ones the person we
once loved is not within there drugs rushing through their veins
no happiness within just the fear of the pain it's hard to watch
someone you love die slowly and there's nothing you can do they
will manipulate and pull on your heart strings that's all they can
do but you have to be strong and not give in even the begging will
be hard to ignore the only wanted something when there at your
door there love has been replaced with a high heartbroken and all
you want to do is cry because you know one day they could take a hit
and die drug addiction is a horrible life could be a family member
or even your wife a mum or dad or a best friend a brother or sister
but there not who they used to be.

A fluttering butterfly landing softly on the grass so delicate and free no cares on the world just colourful and pretty, sea is steady and calm as I sit and stare wondering what life brings for me next what does the universe have In store for me trying to be at ease but my muscles they clench when I have to look up my eyes sting like they've never seen the sun try to fight passed it but it's not enough, people walking by been on there walks sat here alone just trying to be at peace but hearing them talk, clouds look like cotton candy good enough to eat, I think I feel a bit more at ease as I'm tapping my feet, I can hear the crickets chirping as they try to hide in the grass two women chatting and having a laugh, car doors slam and dogs start to bark, it's peaceful but I'm just on edge why do I feel like someone who I know is going to turn up I can feel it in my belly like a burning intense passionate feeling

I finally found why I don't feel free
Because my flat is trying to consume me
Bricks and walls and cement
A place that makes you wonder lust not content
No matter how many times you decorate
You'll never be at peace because the mud and mother earth's energy
is what you need
The green leafs and the roots on a tree
I need to be in nature to feel free

His face consumes my mind never met him but his eyes look kind I dreamt of him I'm drawn like a magnet pulling me in I think it's obsession or is it the unknown the mystery of his looks why is he travelling through my veins like a drug or a disease he doesn't even know I exist I need to know why I'm so intrigued why his face consumes my mind I need to get him out I need to evict

She was like no other she knew her worth she knew how unique she was and that scared them off a wild woman some would exile back in the day but one man one true warrior would see her wildness as beauty and grace

Have you ever wondered what your life would be if you didn't have your children where would you be what would you be doing would you be travelling or would you be lonely on your own with no love from a precious soul and unconditional love I think life would be dull and not sparkle as much I couldn't vision my life without them I wouldn't have a life

His face consumes my mind never met him but his eyes look kind I dreamt of him I'm drawn like a magnet pulling me in I think it's obsession or is it the unknown the mystery of his looks why is he travelling through my veins like a drug or a disease he doesn't even know I exist I need to know why I'm so intrigued why his face consumes my mind I need to get him out I need to evict

Free spirited children do not comply with the normal society's rules they see the world threw their own eyes,
they hear,taste,see,and feel differently
What I have learnt today is a free spirited child has there own boundaries there own rules
they do what they feel that comes naturally to them they could spend an hour playing the piano touching the same keys repetitive sounds,
they might not want to create a masterpiece with the paint maybe just maybe they want to eat it and smell it, to experiment with the paint they really want to understand what the paint is,they see colours they see a science experiment they see texture,they see war paint,crafts with a child is an amazing experience they can teach you loads you see cardboard they see a sword to chop down the forest they've got to get through,
you see wool they see rope to captive there prisoners
,you see junk they see whatever they want to see children being free learn from their imagination there outlook their happy free minds,

I speak to the moon, I give thanks for its light, I give gratitude for having a roof over my head, and beautiful children in my life, grateful for my family and friends, I give thanks to higher power for protecting me at all times, for when my mind becomes blurry I get given a second sight, I'm a beautiful creature that cannot be tamed, you don't have to understand me, I get me and I understand me.

My body aches my soul is weak I have to keep fighting and not admit defeat like a wolf wild and free I'm a mother protecting my pack got to keep moving so they can see that

I'm scared to be around him and look into his eyes, just in case the feeling I feel is real and it sparks the flame inside,
I don't think I'm ready for that ride or die love so I will contain it and continue to hide.

The spark in his eyes as he took my hand we started to dance, like something out of a old film pulled me in close and kissed my lips my mind, body and soul
I forgot all my troubles and started to believe in happiness again for a while

A parent's love

A piece of her heart is
missing this year two souls passed, she has to smile and pretend
she's not broken inside for her children and be happy and laugh,
once again she will put on her mask make Christmas magical and
full of hope and dreams be merry like she didn't cry herself to sleep

In all these years that we've talked my hearts never pine for you so
much, your smell, your kiss and the way your skin feels on mine I
think I've got feelings already please don't be mad, I don't want
to rush I don't want to be in a relationship but I do know I want
you more than you'll ever know one day I may be "your girl"

There once was a man full of love and light tell you stories that makes you feel like the world is alright
walked the earth full of wisdom and sights
Never let anything drag him down rescued himself from the bottle and started to live his life an amazing father when he stepped up children who understood that life wasn't easy it was tough forgive and forget all the mistakes because a parent holds a special place in your heart
He was filled with wonder and didn't see the world in blavk and white he used his vision and created some amazing art he touched the life of some amazing souls with his wisdom and his might he no longer walks the earth and the stories is what we hold onto the memories the strong man full of wisdom broke and decided to take his own life leaving behind his children full of pain my father my hero

What is passion what is love is it from a lover or a story to be told
is it the burning you feel inside your belly
is it the dedication you wish on so many
is it a kind hearted human helping others out
is it a kiss you pine for at night
is it the pain you feel when they walk away
is it the words that just flow or a pen to paper letting your
thoughts go
Is it a beating heart full of life
Is it blood running through your veins
Is it the moment you realise what your doing is great
what is passion what is love someone must know

Tiny grains slip through your fingers and it feels impossible to
hold You may feel contentment you may feel hope
you may even given up with belief whatever you feel is always right
find tranquility in those feelings right or wrong
you need to let your emotions flow
have courage and show unity but most of all don't get too
comfortable show your solidity
be kind to yourself don't forget forgiveness
don't let the whispers pass you by
engage and listen to the positivity within the robustness trying to
break free and comes calling
you're an amazing human in this sad life of illusions your not
fallen as long as you find your peace mind heart and soul you can
live to your full potential be at peace even when your mind's
racing and you feel like there is no hope your soul may be weak
where sand grains used to slip your fingers they no longer
seap,bunched together with water nothing is out of reach
if you build the foundations find solutions to your problems your
soul will be at peace

I am not defined by who you think I am,I'm not defined by the Chinese whispers,i am not defined by the judgement of others,I see the world differently to your Her eyes opened
But her soul was weak She felt like an alien or a walking disease Once full of wisdom and goals to achieve
Her heart felt heavy no longer self love she could feel it whittle away No longer has clarity a clear mind went a stray
But for her children she has unconditional love
Trust's in the future as she walks along a path with hidden meanings As she pulls her strength to fight once more another door closes and another one to explore She grasps it and pulls like withdrawing the sword from the stone Magic begins
beauty shines through it surrounds her like a white glowing cloak wrapped around her body Her grounding armour once more to be seen made of self love and boundaries
Drawing this sword has given her hope sword in hand compassion spills through her pores Her highest self has opened a spiritual door
Full of beliefs in wellbeing and abundance
Prevailing the darkness that held onto her once

Negativity or positivity either way smudge and smudge some more to remove any negativity from your environment and aura

She could cast a spell with just the tone of her voice
The look in her eyes
And the words that rolled of her tongue
For she was all the elements a coven in
one

Ashes

A fire filled stomach full of coal and when I say coal I mean pain
A volcano ready to erupt lava seeping its way up to my throat so I
can't speak I just choke and when I say lava I mean anxiety
Drums beating in my chest like im having cpr
Legs moulded like jelly one step and I could slip, splat on the
floor,
where my body will perish into a thin veil of despair drowning in
the ocean with my own tears
luckily for me I can swim when I say swim I mean fight
It's comfortable down here in this ocean jelly mess
but I am a mother and someone has to clean no time to rest
Drums resuscitate me I take a gasp of air I mould myself together
once more
Climb Mount Everest and when I say Mount Everest I mean floor
One foot at a time
the air gets harder with each step I take
but I remember I'm a Taylor and I will not break

A LANTERN HELPS THE FLAME STAY ALIGHT
LIKE A PARENTS LOVE
PROTECTION TO KEEP THE FIRE WITHIN THEMSELVES

Even in a dark picture the sun breaks through representing light
positivity will always prevail

Look at those eyes she hears it all the time
stay in and meditate to try and hide
Don't release the demons dicing with ure positive soul
Becoming part of the dark side a road no man chooses to go
Infecting YA brain hiding a story only me myself and I know!
Trying to contain!
Walking through the forest all un aware what becomes in the light
but it's near!!

Fed up of failing relationships and not being able to call someone my soul mate my baby
I want it to be right and dont wanna rush
I wanna make sure ure committed like me
Just as much
Love isn't about words and physical stuff
It's about energy and connection and jealousy and anger and lust
it's greed. And it's envy it is the seven deadly sins
I don't want the negatives only the positive
I wanna connect with you on a whole new level
Wanna feel your spiritual vibes wanna see into your soul wanna build a strong foundation that only we will know!!

Children don't remember the labels you put on them
They remember the plasters when they've fallen down
They don't remember the expensive outfits
They remember there frowns being turned around
They don't remember the hundred pound gift u got under tree when there little
They remember the story's at night to get them settled
Don't get me wrong u need money to raise a child but what they need the most is love and a happy parent with a smile

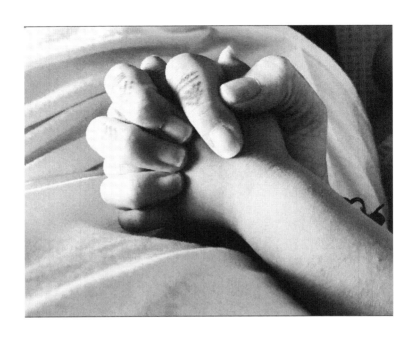

SOMETIMES YOU HAVE TO WRITE YOUR OWN ENDING!!! IT'S A BOOK THAT YOU THOUGHT YOU COULD READ TILL THE END BUT THE TRUTH IS YOU'RE STUCK ON SAME CHAPTER SAME SENTENCES TRYING TO UNDERSTAND TRYING TO VISUALISE IT TRYING TO REACH THE END YOUR FINGERTIPS ARE WEARING OUT THE INK ON THE PAGES BECAUSE YOUR HOLDING ONTO THAT ONE CHAPTER WHEN YOUR JUST GOING TO BE STUCK GOING AROUND IN CIRCLES SAME CHAPTER DIFFERENT DAY

EVERY PICTURE TELLS A STORY

Don't let them sheep rent any space in your head!!! Their problems are not yours, their reflection of you is a reflection of the things they hate about themselves!!!
They will beat you down cause they know you can accomplish anything and they have no dreams don't let them dull your spark baby girl your a soldier

I FEEL THAT SPARK I FEEL THE PAIN IT SHOULDN'T BE LIKE THIS OVER BEFORE ITS BEGAN

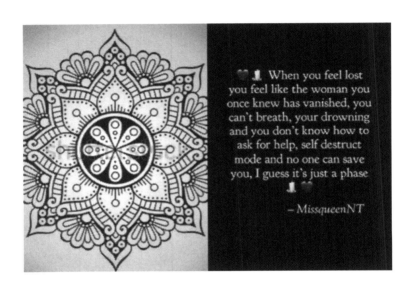

💜⚱️ When you feel lost you feel like the woman you once knew has vanished, you can't breath, your drowning and you don't know how to ask for help, self destruct mode and no one can save you, I guess it's just a phase ⚱️💜

— *MissqueenNT*

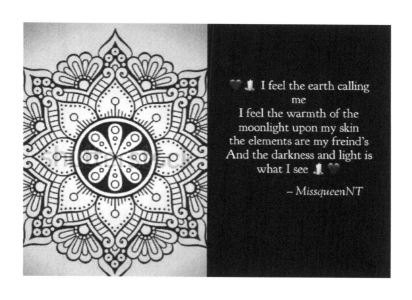

🖤 🕯 I feel the earth calling me
I feel the warmth of the moonlight upon my skin
the elements are my freind's
And the darkness and light is what I see 🕯 🖤

– MissqueenNT

They couldn't handle her wild nature her on and off switch
Misunderstood she never bow'd her head and submitted
She loved to deep for many
She scared the bravest of men
Melted the coldest hearts
But she did not change
She stayed true to herself and her soul
For her soul wasn't like any other it was an old wise soul
Her eyes saw through the lies before they ran off their tongues
She was a warrior
only the bravest souls stayed ready for an axe to reveal their hearts

She pines for freedom
But what is freedom without sacrifice
Is it walking away from loved ones and to travel
Or taking your own life
How to escape reality without taking your soul
How Can you really be free

One thought a day something to be grateful for because sometimes
we forget that the little things make the biggest impacts in our
life's
A smile when you're feeling down
A helping hand or helping someone
A kind word a kind gesture
stay mindful forget yesterday it's gone
don't worry about what tomorrow brings live in the here and now
and be thankful

Pure hearts no knowledge of the world's problems
Their heads full of magic and fairy tales
No pain no worries
Pure imaginations
Just as children should be

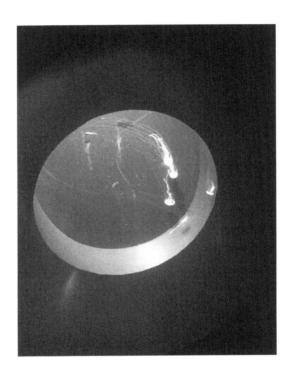

When she chokes and can't express how she feels
she grabs some paper and a pen and all her troubles are written
away

Relying on people is dangerous
there are some people in this world who will take advantage of your
kindness
They are full of pure hate
Never see their actions as bad and pass the blame
It's never there fault always an excuse to why they treat people so
poorly
I always remind myself it's there problems and don't take it
personally
But how can you not feel the let down and the hurt
when you've trusted them with everything you've got
Some people are only there for you when they have something to
gain
If you don't see it straight away you will end up playing in there
little game
Just remember you are a pure soul don't let them break you make
sure you learn from it and grow

Never sit there a wonder if your doing enough easier said than done but everyday without even knowing it you have an impact on people's lives just a smile or hearing your laugh uplifts peoples spirits

As I sit In the sun and passion fills my mind of the unknown and the truth that I'm yet to find I ponder why people don't wanna fight,fight for this world we live in live to make it right and I sit here with these thoughts that are imbedded in my brain I feel sad I feel unhappy and I feel ashamed to be livin in a world that's full of hatred and man made disease and my mind body and soul screams out for peace screams out to be at ease!! But then there's this thing that jumps into my head and makes me forget,makes me forget the passion that runs through my veins. I'm just a girl trapped in this system and I can't be that change.

But u can be that change if u used your mind right u can be that"one" to stand up and fight cause the world mite think ure crazy but u are not alone stand up for what u believe in stand up for what u know open there eyes by touching and reaching her soul you've done it all your life helping others putting people into a positive road Your calling ure life don't sit down and not change it cause that thought that crossed your mind is the fear they want u to feel but u are the master of your own universe it's ure mission to face it!! Stand alone even if u have to but stand up and stand proud and feed your passion and let the world hear u BE LOUD CHANGE IT!!

As you sit here deep in thought, ponder life, ponder what I've been taught, what's my lesson from all this pain, what has my life become, what did I gain?

As I stare at the foggy sky I know a tear wants to leave my eye!! But instead I admire the fog and the view that is blocked the view that's covering my eyes from the distance the distance which is yet unclear

So I'm grateful for the fogginess that covers me!! But I can still see the bare trees that yet hasn't bloomed but I know they will cause there roots hasn't yet been torn there's still life in there there still standing tall no concrete jungle to surround them they stand tall stand proud Mother Earth to ground them! So even on the foggiest days there's still beauty all around u just have to see it captured it and be proud that like that tree u stand tall and proud

I wake up each day thinking where is life taking me
what is my path and at night time I sit down and I laugh
cause another day has gone another day has passed but it wasn't
waisted
I smiled, I was happy and I laughed
So now when I wake up each morning I won't ask that question I
will get up with a smile on my face
and realise this is my path to go with the flow it ain't no race!
To appreciate what I got not what I want not what I need
cause when I die I wouldn't be taking anything with me
apart from my mind body and soul so really that is what matters
that's what life is that's reality
I'm gonna laugh everyday and harder the next concentrate on the
here and now not what's yet to become because if I did that I would
miss out on the here and now miss out on the fun!

I'm grateful for my life and the way it's turning out
I'm walking on my path may be a destructive one but I'm grateful
without a doubt!
Thoughts fill my head but it's okay I'll let them pass through no
room to stay
I'll play this deck that's In front of me! Gamble for what?happiness
and being free
I get down but mostly get up
cause I don't let it fester around too much
I dust it off and come back stronger cause even with this negative
it is a lesson!!!

My father
Your feet make never feel the Earth
but every step I take you will be with me
Every leaf and flower I will think of you
every river and tree I will see you
Every waterfall every wave will be your voice to
comfort me
Every rock and the creatures underneath them
Every animal and bird I will feel your presence
around me
My father
eco-warrior footprints left on mothers earths heart
Everyone of her creations wild and free
every colour every form I know you're with me
R.I.p my father

I hope you are proud of me I completed my book
Alan Taylor
October 16,1960 ---october 2,2020

Printed in Great Britain
by Amazon